the Silent Teaching
a beginner's guide to meditation

Sri Chinmoy

Introduction by Alan Spence

AUM

PUBLICATIONS

Contents

ISBN 0 88497-601-7
Copyright © 1996 Sri Chinmoy

Printed and published by
Aum Publications
86-24 Parsons Blvd.
Jamaica, N.Y. 11432

INTRODUCTION

The title of this collection, 'The Silent Teaching', may at first glance seem strange, even paradoxical. To the mind which is accustomed to regard teaching as instruction, or at best practical demonstration, the notion that such a process can be silent, word-less, may be difficult.

Yet in discussing meditation we are moving in a realm where, traditionally, truth is communicated directly, in silence, by a look, a gesture, a touch. (One of the best known examples is Buddha's 'flower-sermon', in which he came to address a large gathering, and his 'lecture' consisted of holding up a flower!) As Sri Chinmoy puts it, 'All real spiritual masters teach meditation in silence.'

It is not surprising then, that when such masters do use words, the mode is poetic, or paradoxical, or mantric (in which the sound and rhythm of the words actually invoke *the qualities described). The aim is always to by-pass the analytical mind and speak directly to that deeper source of aware-*

ness which Sri Chinmoy calls the heart.

A book by such a master could never be merely a manual, meditation reduced to techniques. (Though you will find a good deal of practical advice in section three of this volume.)

The techniques suggested by Sri Chinmoy are like springboards for the creative use of the imagination. What you can only imagine today, you will one day discover as real, and eventually you can grow into that reality.

He writes, 'You have always to create. This creation of yours is something which you ultimately become. Finally you come to realize that your creation is nothing other than your self-revelation.'

Sri Chinmoy stresses that there is always more to meditation than techniques, useful though they may be. And that 'more' is essentially the seeker's sincere aspiration, the 'inner cry' for the highest.

'Aspiration', he writes, 'is a cry within our heart. The heart is crying and yearning like a mounting flame burning upward.' And this gets to the very heart of his teaching, brings out the essential dynamism of his philosophy. Meditation is not simply a passive process, though openness and receptivity are clearly important. What is also required is a positive, creative approach, the upward movement of aspiration.

'Meditation shows us how we can aspire for something and at the same time how we can achieve it.'

＊ ＊ ＊ ＊ ＊ ＊ ＊ ＊ ＊ ＊ ＊ ＊

*The section of this book dealing with the prac-
ticalities of meditation comes, as indicated, at the
end. The structure, the movement of the book, seems
a natural one: from the inspired mystic vision, to
the articulation of a philosophy, to practical down-
to-earth guidance. It runs the whole range, and
includes a selection from some of his most exalted
writings on the subject. Here he is operating most
clearly in what I described earlier as a 'mantric'
mode. Such passages are scriptural in their inten-
sity, and can leave no doubt in the reader that they
were written (or rather 'delivered', since they are
mostly transcriptions of the spoken word) by a poet
and a master of meditation. They have the true ring
of authenticity and contain their own invitation to
the silence beyond the words.*

*'Meditation is silence, energizing and fulfilling.
Silence is the eloquent expression of the inexpressible.'*

＊ ＊ ＊ ＊ ＊ ＊ ＊ ＊ ＊ ＊ ＊ ＊

*Sri Chinmoy was born in what was then Bengal,
India, in 1931. At an early age he underwent a pro-
found spiritual awakening, attaining a state which
he calls God-realization.*

*He spent some twenty years in an ashram (spiri-
tual community) before coming to the West in 1964.*

5

Since then he has established a number of meditation centres in Europe, Australia and North America, offering what is very much an integral yoga, combining 'the spirituality of the East and the dynamism of the West'.

Although Sri Chinmoy recognizes that 'we can never get meditation from books', at the same time, the words of one who has attained the highest realization can be a tremendous inspiration to those starting out on the journey. For meditation is not something theoretical. It can be thought about, certainly; talked about, yes; but ultimately it has to be practised: 'A theory must be tested. A fact must be honoured. A truth must be lived.'

Alan Spence

THE ABSOLUTE

No mind, no form, I only exist;
　　Now ceased all will and thought.
The final end of Nature's dance,
　　I am It whom I have sought.

A realm of Bliss bare, ultimate;
　　Beyond both knower and known;
A rest immense I enjoy at last;
　　I face the One alone.

I have crossed the secret ways of life,
　　I have become the Goal.
The Truth immutable is revealed;
　　I am the way, the God-Soul.

My spirit aware of all the heights,
　　I am mute in the core of the Sun.
I barter nothing with time and deeds;
　　My cosmic play is done.

Meditation is the eye that sees the Truth, the heart that feels the Truth and the soul that realizes the Truth.

Through meditation the soul becomes fully aware of its evolution in its eternal journey. Through meditation we see the form evolve into the Formless, the finite into the Infinite; and we see the Formless evolve into the form, the Infinite into the finite.

Meditation speaks. It speaks in silence. It reveals. It reveals to the aspirant that matter and spirit are one, quantity and quality are one, the immanent and the transcendent are one. It reveals that life can never be the mere existence of seventy or eighty years between birth and death, but is, rather, Eternity itself. Our birth is a significant incident in God's own existence. And so is our death. In our birth, life lives in the body. In our death, life lives in the spirit.

* * * * * * * * * * * * *

Meditation means conscious self-expansion. Meditation means the recognition or discovery of one's own true self. It is through meditation that we transcend limitations, imperfections and bondage.

Meditation is dynamism on the inner planes of consciousness. When we meditate, what we actually do is enter into the deeper part of our being. At that time, we are able to bring to the fore the wealth that we have deep within us. Meditation shows us how we can aspire for something and, at the same time, how we can achieve it. If we practise meditation daily, then we can rest assured that the problems of our life, inner and outer, are solved.

The spiritual heart is the centre of infinite and universal love. Deep within the heart is the soul, our inner divinity. Meditation in the spiritual heart is the safest and most fulfilling path. In this meditation, we focus all our attention on the heart, silencing the mind, and dive deep within, to ever deeper levels of peace, and bliss, and love. Or, we may use the help of the imagination, and picture a blossom unfolding in our heart. Here, we will feel that as the petals unfold, our inner divinity is radiating through our entire being. We will immerse ourselves in the flow from the heart, and allow it to expand within us, carrying our consciousness to the furthest beyond. In our deepest meditation in the heart, we are far beyond all thought. We are merged in silent communion with the Divine Being, our Beloved. Meditation leads us to conscious identification with our Highest Self.

Meditation is like going to the bottom of the

sea, where everything is calm and tranquil. On the surface there may be a multitude of waves, but the sea is not affected below. In its deepest depths, the sea is all silence. When we start meditating first we try to reach our own inner existence–that is to say, the bottom of the sea. Then, when the waves come from the outside world, we are not affected. Fear, doubt, worry and all the earthly turmoils will just wash away, because inside us is solid peace. Thoughts cannot touch us, because our mind is all peace, all silence, all oneness. Like fish in the sea, they jump and swim but leave no mark. So when we are in our highest meditation we feel that we are the sea, and the animals in the sea cannot affect us. We feel that we are the sky, and all the birds flying past cannot affect us. Our mind is the sky and our heart is the infinite sea. This is meditation. When we want to go high in meditation, then our aspiration is climbing, climbing fearlessly toward the Highest. There is no end to our upward journey because we are travelling in Infinity. We are climbing towards the ever-transcending Beyond. In terms of distance, upward and inward are both infinite journeys toward one Goal, the Supreme. We cannot go high by using the mind, however. We must go through the mind, beyond the mind, and into the realm of the spiritual heart once more. The domain of the spiritual heart is infinitely higher and vaster than that of the highest mind. Far beyond the mind is the domain of the heart. The heart is boundless in every direction, so inside the heart is the highest height as well as the deepest depth.

The higher we can go, the deeper we can go. Again, the deeper we can go, the higher we can go . It works simultaneously. If we can meditate very powerfully, then we are bound to feel that we are going both very high and very deep. Height and depth go together, but they work in two different dimensions, so to speak. But if a person can go very high in his meditation, then he has the capacity to go very deep also.

Before we realize the highest, we feel that there is a difference between height and depth. When we are climbing up, we will feel that we have reached a certain height, and when we are diving deep within, we will feel that we have reached a certain depth. But height and depth are all in the mental consciousness. Once we go beyond the barrier of the mind and enter into the Universal Consciousness, we see everything as one and inseparable. At that time only Reality is singing and dancing within us, and we become the Reality itself. It has no height, no depth, no length. It is all one and at the same time it is all the time transcending its own limits.

In meditation there is a flame of constant aspiration. Our journey is eternal; our progress and our realization are also constant and unending because we are dealing with Infinity, Eternity and Immortality.

Meditation is man's thirst for the Infinite Real, Eternal Real and Absolute Real. The secret of meditation is to achieve conscious and constant oneness with God. The secret supreme of meditation is to feel God as one's very own, and finally to realize God for God's sake, Him to reveal and Him to fulfil.

Meditation is self-transcendence. Self-transcendence is the message of the Beyond. The message of the Beyond is God the eternally evolving Soul, and God, the eternally fulfilling Goal.

Meditation tells you only one thing: God *is*. Meditation reveals to you only one truth: yours is the vision of God

* * * * * * * * * * * * *

Meditation is silence, energizing and fulfilling. Silence is the eloquent expression of the inexpressible.

What is the first and foremost thing we expect from meditation? Peace. Peace and nothing else.

Peace is the beginning of love. Peace is the completion of truth. Peace is the return to the Source.

Meditation, like the wings of a bird, is always expanding into Peace, Light and Delight.

Meditation alone can give birth to perfection. Meditation carries us beyond the frustration of the senses, beyond the limitation of the reasoning mind. And, finally, meditation can present us with the breath of perfection.

* * * * * * * * * * * * *

Meditation helps us to live from moment to moment. Again, in moment to moment the Eternal Now exists. The Eternal cannot be separated from each moment. This is a moment and here Eternity is all around. Eternity comprises the present, the past and the future.

Inside Eternity is the moment; again, inside the moment is Eternity. It is like the ocean. Inside the ocean are countless tiny drops. Again, each tiny drop holds the essence of the vast ocean. We take a drop and immediately we have the consciousness of the vast ocean, because the drop embodies the vast ocean. And so each moment cannot be separated from Eternity and Infinity. Meditation is the only way to feel the oneness of the finite with the Infinite.

Does meditation encourage us to escape from reality? No! On the contrary, meditation inspires us to accept God's creation as an unmistakable reality that still awaits transformation and perfection. When the earth-consciousness is transformed, and our body-consciousness is transformed, only then can we be true receptacles of the infinite Truth and infinite Light. He who meditates has to act like a divine hero amidst humanity. Humanity is part and parcel of God. By throwing aside humanity, how are we going to reach divinity? We have to accept the world as it is now. If we don't accept a thing, how can we transform it? If a potter does not touch the lump of clay how is he going to shape it into a pot? The world around us is not perfect, but we also are not perfect. Perfect Perfection has not yet dawned. We have to know that humanity at present is far, far from perfection. But we are also members of that humanity. How are we going to discard our brothers and sisters who are our veritable limbs? I cannot discard my arm. It is impossible. Similarly, when we meditate soulfully, devotedly, we have to accept humanity as our very own. We have to take it with us. If we are in a position to inspire others, if we are one step ahead, then we have the opportunity to serve the divinity in the ones who are following us.

So we must not enter into the Himalayan caves. We have to face the world here and now. We have to transform the face of the world on the strength of our dedication to the divinity in humanity. Meditation is not an escape. Meditation is the acceptance of life in its totality with a view to transforming it for the highest manifestation of the divine Truth here on earth.

WHEN

When he concentrates,
    Everything matters.
When he meditates,
    Nothing matters.
When he contemplates,
    Only God matters.

If we feel that we are satisfied with what we have and what we are, then there is no need for us to enter the field of meditation. The reason we enter into meditation is because we have an inner hunger. We feel that within us there is something luminous, something vast, something divine. We feel that we need this thing very badly; only right now we do not have access to it. So our hunger comes from our spiritual need.

Meditation does not mean just sitting quietly for five or ten minutes. It requires conscious effort. The mind has to be made calm and quiet; at the same time, it has to be vigilant so as not to allow any distracting thoughts or desires to enter. When we can make the mind calm and quiet, we will feel that a new creation is dawning inside us. When the mind is vacant and tranquil and our whole existence becomes an empty vessel, our inner being can invoke infinite Peace, Light and Bliss to enter into the vessel and fill it. This is meditation.

When we think that it is we who are trying to meditate, then meditation seems complicated. But real meditation is not done by us. It is done by our inner Pilot, the Supreme, who is constantly meditating in and through us. We are just the vessel, and we are allowing Him to fill us with His whole Consciousness. We start with our own personal effort, but once we go deep within, we see that it is not our effort that is allowing us to enter into meditation. It is the Supreme who is meditating in and through us with our conscious awareness and consent.

* * * * * * * * * * * *

Meditation has to be practised spontaneously, soulfully and correctly. If it is not, dark doubt will blight your mind and utter frustration will steal into your heart. And you will probably find your whole existence thrown into the depths of a yawning chasm.

For meditation you need inspiration. Scriptures can supply you with inspiration. To buy a spiritual book takes ten seconds. To read that book takes a few hours. To absorb that book takes a few years. And to live the truths thereof may take not only a whole lifetime, but a few incarnations.

For meditation you need aspiration. The presence, physical or spiritual, of a spiritual teacher can awaken your sleeping aspiration. He can awaken your sleeping aspiration. He can easily and will gladly do it for you. Aspiration: this is precisely what you need in order to reach your journey's goal. You don't have to worry about your realization. Your aspiration will take care of it.

If you have a teacher who is a realized soul, his silent gaze will teach you how to meditate. A Master does not have to explain outwardly how to meditate or give you a specific form of meditation. He will simply meditate on you and inwardly teach you how to meditate. Your soul will enter into his soul and learn from his soul. All real spiritual Masters teach meditation in silence.

When a realized spiritual master enters into his highest consciousness, he is one with the Divinity within him. The human individual is entirely merged with the Supreme. At this time, the master's consciousness is a direct access to the Light which a meditator is searching to uncover in his own heart. The master's consciousness reveals and offers what the seeker has been working to find deep within himself. To identify with the highest meditation of the master is to have direct experience of the consciousness which is the Goal of one's inner search. This is not meditation on a human individual, but rather meditation on the Divine Consciousness, which is using the man as an instrument to reveal itself.

* * * * * * * * * * * *

The heart is the seat of the soul. The Source and the Reality are in the heart.

As you concentrate on anything —a picture, a flower, a flame — so also can you concentrate on the heart.

What concentration can do in our day-to-day life is unimaginable. Concentration is the surest way to reach your goal. It is concentration that acts like an arrow and enters into the target.

> Concentration is the Arrow.
> Meditation is the Bow.

When you concentrate, you focus all your energies upon the chosen phenomenon in order to unveil its mysteries. When you meditate, you rise into a higher consciousness.

Concentration wants to penetrate into the object it strives for. Meditation wants to live in the vastness of Silence.

In concentration, you endeavour to bring the consciousness of your object right into your own awareness. In meditation, you rise from your limited consciousness into a higher and wider domain.

If you want to sharpen your faculties, concentrate. If you want to lose yourself, meditate.

It is the work of concentration to clear the roads when meditation wants to go either deep within or high above.

Concentration wants to seize the knowledge it aims at. Meditation wants to identify itself with the knowledge it seeks for.

* * * * * * * * * * * * *

Concentration means inner vigilance and alertness. There are thieves all around us and within us. Fear, doubt, worry and anxiety are inner thieves that are trying to steal our inner poise and peace of mind. When we learn how to concentrate, it is very difficult for these hostile forces to enter into us. If doubt enters into our mind, the power of concentration will tear doubt to pieces. If fear enters into our mind, the power of concentration will chase away our fear. Right now we are victims to unlit, obscure, destructive thoughts, but a day will come when, on the strength of our concentration, disturbing thoughts will be afraid of us.

Concentration is the mind's dynamic will that operates in us for our acceptance of light and rejection of darkness. It is like a divine warrior in us. What concentration can do in our life of aspiration is unimaginable. It can easily separate Heaven from hell, so that we can live in the constant delight of Heaven and not in the perpetual worries, anxieties and tortures of hell while we are here on earth.

When we concentrate, we are like a bullet entering into something or we are like a magnet pulling the object of concentration toward us. At that time, we do not allow any thought to enter into our mind, whether it is divine or undivine, earthly or heavenly, good or bad. In concentration the entire mind has to be focused on a particular object or subject. If we are concentrating on the petal of a flower, we try to feel that nothing else exists in the entire world but us and the petal. We look neither forward nor backward, upward nor inward; only we try to pierce the object with our one-pointed concentration. But this is not an aggressive way of looking into a thing or entering into an object. Far from it! This concentration comes directly from the soul's indomitable will, or will power.

* * * * * * * * * * * *

Very often I hear aspirants say that they cannot concentrate for more than five minutes.

After five minutes they get a headache or their head is on fire. Why? It is because the power of their concentration is coming from the intellectual mind or, you can say, the disciplined mind. The mind knows that it must not wander; that much knowledge the mind has. But if the mind is to be utilized properly, in an illumined way, then the light of the soul has to come into it. When the light of the soul has entered into the mind, it is extremely easy to concentrate on something for hours and hours. During this time there can be no thoughts or doubts or fears. No negative forces can enter into the mind if it is surcharged with the soul's light.

So when we concentrate, we try to feel that the soul's light is coming from the heart and passing through the third eye. Then, with this light, we enter into the object of concentration and identify with it. The final stage of concentration is to discover the hidden ultimate truth in the object of concentration.

* * * * * * * * * * * * *

When we concentrate, we focus our attention on one particular thing. But when we meditate, we feel that we have the capacity deep within us to see many things, deal with many things and welcome many things all at the same time. When we meditate, we try to expand ourselves, like a bird spreading its wings. We try to expand our finite consciousness and enter into the universal Consciousness where there is no fear, jealousy or doubt but only joy, peace and divine power.

Meditation means our conscious growth into the Infinite. When we meditate, what we actually do is enter into a vacant, calm, silent mind and allow ourselves to be nourished and nurtured by Infinity itself.

Through concentration we become one-pointed and through meditation we expand our consciousness into the Vast and enter into *its* consciousness. But in contemplation we grow into the Vast itself, and its consciousness becomes our very own. In contemplation we are at once in our deepest concentration and our highest meditation. The Truth that we have seen and felt in meditation, we grow into and become totally one with in contemplation. When we are concentrating on God, we may feel God right in front of us or beside us. When we are meditating, we are bound to feel Infinity, Eternity and Immortality within us. But when we are contemplating, we will see that we ourselves are God, that we ourselves are Infinity, Eternity and Immortality.

Contemplation means our conscious oneness with the infinite, eternal Absolute. Here the Creator and the creation, the lover and the beloved, the knower and the thing known become one. One moment we are the divine lover and God is the Supreme Beloved. The next moment we change roles. In contemplation, we become one with the Creator and see the whole universe inside us. At that time, when we look at our own existence we don't see a human being. We see something like a dynamo of Light, Peace and Bliss.

If we meditate on a specific divine quality in an unshaped form such as Light or Peace or Bliss, or if we meditate in an abstract way on Infinity, Eternity or Immortality, then all the time we will feel an express train going forward inside us. We are meditating on Peace, Light or Bliss while the express train is constantly moving. Our mind is calm and quiet in the vastness of Infinity, but there is a movement; a train is going endlessly toward our goal. We are envisioning a goal and meditation is taking us there.

In contemplation it is not like that. In contemplation, the entire universe and farthest Goal we feel deep inside ourselves. When we are contemplating, we feel that we are holding within ourselves the entire universe with all its infinite Light, Peace, Bliss and Truth. There is no thought, no form, no idea. Everything is merged in contemplation; it is all one stream of consciousness. In our highest contemplation we feel that we are nothing but Consciousness itself; we are one with the Absolute. But in our highest meditation there is a dynamic movement. That movement is not aggressive; we are not beating or striking anyone. Far from it! But a dynamic movement is going on in our consciousness. We are fully aware of what is happening in the inner and the outer world, but we are not affected. In contemplation we are also unaffected by what is going on in the inner and outer world. But there we and our whole existence have become part and parcel of the universe, which we are holding deep inside us.

So concentration gives the message of alertness, meditation gives the message of vastness and contemplation gives the message of inseparable oneness. We concentrate because we want to reach the Goal. We meditate because we want to live in the heart of the Goal. We contemplate

32

because we want to become the Goal.

We concentrate with the mind's illumining one-pointedness. We meditate with the heart's expanding vastness. We contemplate with the soul's fulfilling oneness.

* * * * * * * * * * * * *

At the beginning of our spiritual journey, we feel that meditation is self-effort and perspiration. At the end of our journey's close, we realize that meditation is God's Grace, His Compassion Infinite.

The price is never right. Before realization, it is too high. After realization, it is too low. For a beginner, meditation *is* the highest reality. But when one becomes an advanced seeker one knows that meditation only *leads* to the highest reality. If someone has been for a long time in ignorance, if he has never prayed in his whole life even for a minute, for him meditation is naturally the highest reality that his consciousness may achieve. But when he has practised meditation for a couple of years, he knows that meditation itself is not the highest reality. The highest reality is something he achieves or grows into when he walks along the path of meditation.

We have to start our journey with inspiration. We have to feel every day deep within us in all our activities the necessity of inspiration. Without inspiration there can be no proper achievement. Then we have to go one step further. After inspiration we have to feel the momentous necessity of aspiration. Inspiration is not all. We have to aspire to reach the Golden All, to see the Golden Shores of the Beyond, the ever-transcending Beyond. This is what we expect from aspiration, the mounting flame within us.

But aspiration is not enough, either. We have to meditate. Aspiration includes meditation. When we meditate, we have to feel that we are entering into Infinity, Eternity and Immortality. These are not vague terms, but our true possessions. To someday enter into our own divine possessions —Infinity, Eternity and Immortality — is our birthright. Then, when we become advanced in our meditation, when meditation starts offering us its fruit, we enter the realm of realization. We realize the highest Truth in this body, here on earth. We do not have to go elsewhere to realize God. We do not have to enter a Himalayan cave or sit on a snowcapped mountain in order to practise spirituality. No. Here on earth, in the hustle and bustle of life, we have to practise spirituality. We have to accept earth as it stands, as it is.

If we are afraid of earth, if we shy away from earth, then God-Realization will always remain a far cry. Here on earth we have to realize the highest Truth.

EVER THE SAME AGAIN

Ever the same again
My lost Truth rediscovered.
Ever the same again.

Ever the same again
My forgotten Self remembered.
Ever the same again.

Ever the same again
My lost Goal regained.
Ever the same again.

AUM PUBLICATIONS
86-10 Parsons Blvd.
Jamaica, NY 11432

Dear Friend,

Thank you for your interest in the writings of Sri Chinmoy.

So that we can evaluate our book distribution program, would you kindly fill out the questionnaire below? *(Please print clearly)*

Title of book _____

_____

_____

Where was book bought? *(name of store or if online from which vendor)*

_____

We would be grateful for your comments _____

_____

_____

_____

❏ Please send me your latest catalogue.

Name _____

Address _____

City_____State_____

Zip Code _____ Country _____

❏ Please send a catalogue to my friend listed below:

Name _____

Address _____

City_____State_____

Zip Code _____ Country _____

For more information about Sri Chinmoy's books kindly visit www.srichinmoybooks.com or www.srichinmoylibrary.com

Thank you

BEGINNING

From the spiritual point of view, you have to know that every seeker is a beginner. A beginner is he who has the inner urge to grow into something ever more divine, ever more illumining and ever more fulfilling. The moment you want to make constant and and continuous progress, the moment you want to constantly surpass yourself and enter into the ever-transcending Beyond, at that moment you become an eternal beginner.

If you are an absolute beginner, then you have to start by reading a few spiritual books or scriptures. These will give you inspiration. But you should read books by spiritual Masters in whom you have implicit faith. There *are* Masters who have attained the highest consciousness and if you read their books you are bound to get inspiration.

Only those who have realized the Truth will have the capacity to offer the Truth. Otherwise, it is the blind leading the blind.

In the beginning you should not even think about meditation. Just try to set aside a certain time of day when you will try to be calm and quiet, and feel that these five minutes belong to your inner being and to nobody else. Regularity is of paramount importance. What you need is regular practice at a regular time.

The best way to begin to learn how to meditate is to associate with people who have been meditating for some time. These people are not in a position to teach you, but they are in a position to inspire you. If you have some friends who know how to meditate, just sit beside them while they are meditating. Unconsciously your inner being will be able to derive some meditative power from them. You are not stealing anything from them, but your inner being is taking help from them without your outer knowledge.

The most important thing is practice. Today your mind acts like a monkey. It is knocking all the time at your heart's door and disturbing the poise of the heart. But as many times as the mind comes to you, just chase it away or deliberately place your conscious awareness on something else.

THE ABCs

Let me start with the ABCs of meditation. When you meditate at home, you should have a corner of your room which is absolutely pure and sanctified–a sacred place which you use only for meditation. Here on your shrine you will keep a picture of your spiritual Master, or the Christ, or some other beloved spiritual figure whom you regard as your Master. Those who are my disciples will have my Transcendental picture, in which I am absolutely one with my inner Pilot.

When you are doing your individual daily meditation, try to meditate all alone. This rule does not apply to husband and wife if they have the same spiritual Master; it is all right for them to meditate together. Also, close spiritual friends who understand each other thoroughly in their inner lives can meditate together. Otherwise, it is not advisable to meditate with others during your daily individual meditation. Collective meditation is also important, but for individual daily meditation it is better to meditate privately at one's own shrine.

OUTER AIDS TO MEDITATION

Before beginning to meditate, it is helpful if you can take a shower or proper bath. The purification of the body is absolutely necessary for the purification of the consciousness. If you are unable to take a shower or bath before sitting down to meditate, you should at least wash your face and your feet. It is also advisable to wear clean and light clothes.

It will help if you burn incense and keep some flowers in front of you. There are some people who say that it is not necessary to have flowers around during meditation. They say, 'The flower is inside; the thousand-petalled lotus is inside.' But the physical flower that you have in front of you reminds you of the inner flower. Its colour, its fragrance and its pure consciousness gives you a little inspiration. From inspiration you get aspiration, and from aspiration you get realization.

It is the same with using candles during meditation. The flame from a candle will not in itself give you aspiration; it is the inner flame that will give you aspiration. But when you see the outer flame, then immediately you feel that the flame in your inner being is also climbing high, higher, highest. And when you smell the scent of incense, you get perhaps only an iota of inspiration and purification, but this iota can be added to your inner treasure. If someone is on the verge of God-realization or has actually realized God, then these outer things will have no value. But if you know that God-realization is still a far cry, then they will definitely increase your aspiration.

THE HOUR OF MEDITATION

The best hour for meditation, according to Indian seers, sages and spiritual Masters, is between three and four o'clock in the morning. That is called *Brahma Muhurta*, the time of the Brahman, the best time. But here in the West, if you go to bed late, the best hour for you is five-thirty or six in the morning. The precise hour is to be settled according to the individual case and the individual capacity.

Now, that is the first time in the day. If you can meditate again between twelve and twelve-thirty, for ten or fifteen minutes, it is wonderful. This meditation you have to do inside, not in the street. A day will come when you will be able to meditate anywhere, while driving or doing anything else, but now it is advisable to meditate indoors, in a proper place.

Then, when the sun is about to set, you can look at the sun and meditate. For ten minutes try to meditate. At that time, please try to feel that you have become totally one with the sun, with the cosmic nature. You have played your part during the day most satisfactorily and now you are going to retire. That will be your feeling.

Then meditate when you retire for the night — whenever you go to bed. It is always better to go to bed by eleven o'clock at night. But necessity knows no law; if you are compelled to work at night, it is all right for you.

POSTURE

When meditating, it is important to keep the spine straight and erect, and to keep the body relaxed. When the body is stiff, naturally the divine and fulfilling qualities that are flowing in and through it during meditation will not be received. The body should not be uncomfortable either. When it feels uncomfortable, automatically it will change its position. While you are meditating, your inner being will spontaneously take you to a comfortable position, and then it is up to you to maintain it. The main advantage of the lotus position is that it helps keep the spinal cord straight and erect. But it will not necessarily keep the body relaxed. So the lotus position is not at all necessary for proper meditation. Many people meditate very well while they are seated in a chair.

Some seekers like to meditate while lying down, but I wish to say that this is not at all advisable for the beginner, nor even for those who have been meditating for several years. It is only for the most advanced seekers and for realized souls. Others who try to meditate while lying down will enter into the world of sleep or into a kind of inner drift or doze. Furthermore, while you are lying down, your breathing is not as satisfactory as it is when you are in a sitting position, since it is not conscious or controlled.

My disciples often ask me if they should meditate with their eyes open. Here I wish to say that in ninety out of one hundred cases, disciples who keep their eyes closed during meditation fall asleep. For five minutes they meditate, and then for fifteen minutes they remain in the world of sleep. There is no dynamic energy, but only lethargy and self-complacency, and they feel a kind of restful, sweet sensation. Then, after some time, by God's miraculous Grace they come back again and meditate for two or three minutes.

Actually, it is best to meditate with the eyes partly open and partly closed. In this way you are the root of the tree and at the same time the topmost bough. The part of you that has the eyes half-open feels that it is the root, symbolizing Mother Earth. The other part, which has the eyes half-closed, is the topmost branch, the world of vision or, let us say, Heaven. Your consciousness is on the highest level and it is also here on earth, trying to transform the world.

When you meditate with your eyes half open and half closed, you are doing what is called the lion's meditation. Even while you are going deep within, you are focusing your conscious atten-

BREATHING

Proper breathing is very important in meditation. When breathing, try to breathe in as slowly and quietly as possible, so that if somebody placed a tiny thread in front of your nose it would not move at all. And when you breathe out, try to breathe out even more slowly than when you breathed in. If possible, leave a short pause between the end of your first exhalation and the beginning of your second inhalation. If you can, hold your breath for a few seconds. But if it is difficult, do not do it. Never do anything that will harm your organs or respiratory system.

The first thing that you have to think of when breathing is purity. When you breathe in, if you can feel that the breath is coming directly from God, from Purity itself, then your breath can easily be purified.

Then, each time you breathe in, try to feel that you are bringing into your body peace, infinite peace. The opposite of peace is restlessness. When you breathe out, try to feel that you are expelling the restlessness within you and also the restlessness that you see all around you. When you breathe this way, you will find restlessness leaving you. After practising this for a few times, please try to feel that you are breathing in power from the universe. And when you exhale, feel that all your fear is coming out of your body. After doing this a few times, try to feel that what you are breathing in is joy, infinite joy, and what you are breathing out is sorrow, suffering and melancholy

There is another thing that you can also try. Feel that you are breathing in not air but cosmic energy. Feel that tremendous cosmic energy is entering into you with each breath and that you are going to use it to purify your body, vital, mind and heart. Feel that there is not a single place in your body that is not being occupied by the flow of cosmic energy. It is flowing like a river inside you, washing and purifying your whole being. Then, when you start to breathe out, feel that you are breathing out all the rubbish inside you — all your undivine thoughts, obscure ideas and impure actions. Anything inside your system that you call undivine, anything that you do not want to claim as your own, feel that you are exhaling. This is not the traditional yogic *pranayama*, which is more complicated and systematized, but it is the most effective spiritual method of breathing.

If you practise this method of breathing, you will soon see its results. In the beginning you will have to use your imagination, but after a while you will see and feel that it is not imagination at all but reality. You are consciously breathing in the energy which is flowing all around you, purifying yourself and emptying yourself of everything undivine. If you can breathe this way for five minutes every day, you will be able to make very fast progress. But it has to be done in a very conscious way, not mechanically.

MANTRA

Mantra is a Sanskrit word. In Indian philosophy, spirituality and the inner life, *mantras* play a considerable role. A *mantra* is a syllable divinely surcharged with power.

If you cannot enter into your deepest meditation because your mind is restless, this is an opportunity to utilize a *mantra*. You can repeat 'Supreme' or 'AUM' or 'God' for a few minutes.

The most powerful of all *mantras* is AUM; it is the mother of all *mantras*. AUM is a single, indivisible sound; it is the vibration of the Supreme. AUM is the seed sound of the universe, for with this sound God set into motion the first vibration of His creation. Every second, God is creating Himself anew inside AUM.

Without birth is AUM, without death is AUM. AUM and nothing else existed, exists and will exist. It is best to chant AUM out loud, so its sound can vibrate even in your physical ears and permeate your entire body. This will convince your outer mind and give you a greater sense of joy and achievement. When chanting out loud, the 'M' sound should last at least three times as long as the 'AU' sound. There are many ways to chant AUM. If you chant loudly, you feel the omnipotence of the Supreme. When you chant it softly, you feel the delight of the Supreme. When you chant it silently, you feel the peace of the Supreme.

MUSIC

In the spiritual world, next to meditation is music, the breath of music. Silence is the source of everything. It is the source of music and it is music itself. Silence is the nest and music is the bird.

* * * * * * * * * * * *

Let us not try to understand music with our mind. Let us not even try to feel it with our heart. Let us simply and spontaneously allow the music-bird to fly in our heart-sky.

* * * * * * * * * * * *

Each individual has his own music, each movement has its own music, each action has its own music. Each time we breathe in and breathe out, there is music.

* * * * * * * * * * * *

Music and the spiritual life go together; one complements the other. Music helps the spiritual seeker to go deep within to get the utmost satisfaction from life, from truth, from reality.

* * * * * * * * * * * *

When we listen to soulful music, or when we ourselves play soulful music, immediately our inner existence climbs up high, higher, highest. A river is flowing through us, a river of consciousness, and this consciousness is all the time illumined.

* * * * * * * * * * * *

The best way to become one with soulful music is to have the firm inner conviction that while you are breathing in, the breath is immediately entering directly into your soul. And with the breath, you have to feel that the Universal Consciousness, divine Reality, divine Truth is also entering. Then, when you breathe out, try to feel that you are breathing out the ignorance that is covering your soul. Feel that the veils of ignorance are being lifted and discarded. If you can consciously imagine and feel this, it is the best way to become one with soulful music.

* * * * * * * * * * * *

Singing is a form of meditation. If you cannot carry a tune, no harm. Then you will not sing in public. But certainly you can sing when you are alone. Even if the tune is wrong, if you sing soulfully, it is a real form of meditation.

Meditation and singing are of the same height, provided you sing soulfully. Meditation is of utmost importance and by singing spiritual songs you are getting the opportunity to meditate in the easiest way. This opportunity is knocking at your door at every moment. At every moment you may not like to meditate, but who does not like to carry a tune? If you can sing soulfully, your singing will be considered as good as your meditation. Perhaps if you sing soulfully you will do better than your own meditation.

THE MIND AND THE HEART — SOME EXERCISES

Separate yourself from the mind and observe the mind. You can read hundreds of pages or talk to hundreds of people, but you will not get illumination. So when you think of what the mind has given you, think at the same time of the thing that you really need most and you will see that the mind has not fulfilled this need. Since your mind has disappointed you, why should you concentrate there?

If you meditate in the mind, you will be able to meditate for perhaps five minutes, and out of that five minutes, for one minute you may meditate very powerfully. First you get joy and satisfaction, but then you may feel a barren desert. If you meditate in the heart, a day will come when you start getting satisfaction. If you meditate in the heart, you are meditating where the soul is. True, the light, the consciousness of the soul permeates the whole body, but there is a specific place where the soul resides most of the time, and that is in the heart. I am not speaking of the human heart, the physical heart, which is just another organ. I am speaking of the pure heart, the spiritual heart. The spiritual heart is located in the centre of the chest, in the centre of our existence. If you want illumination you will get that illumination from the soul, which is inside the heart.

When you are trying to make your mind calm and quiet, you are concentrating. When you are successful in chasing away all thoughts that disturb your mind sooner or later your inner self will automatically come to the fore and stand right in front of you like a blazing sun clearing away the veil of clouds. Right now the inner sun is overcast with clouds: thoughts, ideas, doubts, fears and so forth. Take the mind as a monkey or an unruly child. As many times as it comes to you, chase it away or deliberately place your conscious awareness on something else. If you allow it to distract you, it will gain strength and continue to torture you. During your meditation your mind may resist and obstruct you, but you have to feel that you have something superior to the mind, and that is your heart. Just throw the mind and all its possessions into the heart.

* * * * * * * * * * * *

As you concentrate on anything — a picture, a candle, a flame, any material object — so also can you concentrate on the heart. You cannot look physically at your spiritual heart, but you can focus all your attention on it. Then, gradually, the power of your concentration enters into the heart and takes you completely out of the realm of the mind.

Try to breathe in as slowly and as quietly as possible, so that if you placed a tiny thread in front of your nose it would not even move. Then you will see that your meditation will be deep and your mind will be very calm and quiet.

Then imagine something very vast, calm and quiet. When you start meditating, feel that inside you is a vast ocean and that you have dived to the bottom, where it is all tranquillity. If you can identify yourself with this vast ocean, with this flood of tranquillity, then it will be extremely easy for you to meditate.

* * * * * * * * * * * * *

Keep your eyes half open and imagine the vast sky. In the beginning try to feel that the sky is in front of you; later try to feel that you are as vast as the sky, or that you are the vast sky itself. After a few minutes, please close your eyes and try to see and feel the sky inside your heart. Please feel that you are the universal Heart, and that inside you is the sky that you meditated upon and identified yourself with. The universal

MEDITATING ON THE MASTER

If you want to be under the guidance of a spiritual Master, the Master's silent gaze will teach you how to meditate. The Master does not have to explain outwardly how to meditate or give you a special form of meditation or a mantra. He will simply meditate on you and inwardly teach you how to meditate.

When we meditate in front of the picture of a spiritual Master, we should try always to identify ourselves with the consciousness of the spiritual Master which is embodied in the particular picture. If we want to identify ourselves with his consciousness, then the first thing we have to do is concentrate on the whole picture. Gradually, we should bring our focus of attention to only the face, then to between the eyebrows and a little above, which is where his actual inner, spiritual wealth can be found. This is the third eye, the place of vision, and the moment we can identify ourselves with the vision of inner reality, we shall achieve the greatest success. If you want to get purity as you look at the picture, imagine that you are breathing in simultaneously with the Master before you start your meditation.

Feel that the entire picture is ready to give you whatever you want. If you want Peace, then try to look at the picture with the inner feeling that the picture has infinite Peace. If you want Light, if you want Bliss or if you want any divine quality, just feel that the picture has it, which is absolutely true. When you start, you have to imagine that this picture has what you want. Then when you go deep within, you will find the reality.

BEYOND SPEECH AND MIND

Beyond speech and mind,
Into the river of ever-effulgent Light
My heart dives.
Today thousands of doors,
Closed for millennia,
Are opened wide.